CARL LAFERTON

RESCUING CHRISTMAS

THE SEARCH FOR JOY
THAT LASTS

thegoodbook
COMPANY

Rescuing Christmas
© The Good Book Company, 2017.

Published by
The Good Book Company
Tel (UK): 0333 123 0880
Tel (North America): (1) 866 244 2165
International: +44 (0) 208 942 0880
Email (UK): info@thegoodbook.co.uk
Email (North America): info@thegoodbook.com

Websites
UK & Europe: www.thegoodbook.co.uk
North America: www.thegoodbook.com
Australia: www.thegoodbook.com.au
New Zealand: www.thegoodbook.co.nz

ISBN: 9781784982683 | Printed in the UK

Design by André Parker

CONTENTS

For Benjamin and Abigail —
Christmas is much more fun with you around.

LYING AWAKE AND LOOKING FOR BATTERIES

The minutes between Christmas Eve and Christmas Day crawl past like hours when you're a child.

Time staggers as you lie there, sleep refusing to come, waiting for the presents and the food and the fun. I remember lying awake in the dark for hours at a time, only to check the clock on my bedside table and discover that three or (if I had been incredibly disciplined) four minutes had unwound since I last looked at it.

It took days that night to get to the morning. But it was always worth the wait.

It's a magical time, Christmas, for many adults as well as for most children. It's a day of great enjoyment—the highlight of the year. Everything is fun and friendship and feasting (and everyone knows calories don't count in December). We can hit pause on the real world and just enjoy the day. The commercials confirm it: Christmas is the most wonderful time of the year. As one advert from Harrods, the famous upmarket store in the middle of London, put it:

> *Rejoice, Christmas is coming to Harrods, joyful and triumphant in a blaze of celestial splendour ... brimming full of comfort and joy, overflowing with grandeur and gifts.*

Brimming full of comfort and joy. We'll be happy once we get to Christmas.

TIME MOVES QUICKER

The night before Christmas Day moves much faster when you're a parent. The hours skip past like minutes as you try to do all the jobs you should have done earlier in December, but left till Christmas Eve.

Two years ago, we lived through the now-famous (in my head) "Year of the Missing Batteries". Shortly before the shops closed, I discovered that while we had a vast variety of batteries in our home, the only type we did not possess was the type we needed to make one of the kids' presents work; and that the digital camera on which we'd take our Christmas photos had no memory card. I duly raced to our local store.

I assumed that I would be the only person in the shop, but it was heaving with similarly tense, desperate battery-hunters, along with the still more tense and considerably more desperate spouse-present-hunters. (The present-hunters made me feel better about myself—I may have failed to get the batteries, but they had failed to get the actual gifts.)

With a rush of relief I found my memory card and batteries. As I left, I smiled triumphantly at a man who had the unmistakable look of a husband who has been told several times by his wife what she wants for Christmas, and is now wishing he'd actually listened. But I had relaxed too soon. The next few hours at home were spent trying—and failing—to put together the wooden playhouse we'd bought the kids, and whose instructions proved about as much help as suncream in a snowstorm.

I do love Christmas. But at the same time, I sometimes find myself just wanting to get through Christmas Day intact and out the other side, back to normal life. Maybe you're the same. You find Christmas as stressful as you find it joyful. There's the stress of who you'll be with at Christmas, and who you'll disappoint. There's the stress of getting the presents (and batteries). There's the stress of how much food to buy, and when to put it in the oven, and trying to remember whether or not your auntie is still a vegan. And you find yourself thinking, "If I can just get through Christmas, then things will go back to normal".

Maybe, though, you'd love to have that kind of stress. You'd love to have a choice of where to spend Christmas, people to buy presents for at Christmas and guests to cook for over Christmas. But you don't. Perhaps Christmas is a day that produces the opposite of joy. It just reminds you of who you've lost or who you've never had, or of what you'd hoped to achieve or change this year but never did. Maybe this year, for very good reason, you're aiming simply to get through Christmas.

JOY IN JANUARY

When it comes to Christmas, all of us are "get to-ers" or "get through-ers". And the truth is that neither leads to a joy that lasts. There's no joy in getting through, and even if you're a get to-er and Christmas Day, when it comes, feels perfect... well, you still face the adult version of what as a child I came to know as the "4 o'clock feeling". It's the feeling you get when you realise that it is all almost over, and that the day you've looked forward to getting to is now a day that you're looking back on. It's the feeling you get as you slide back into normality and make the annual discovery that the calories did, in fact, count in December.

The problem with Christmas is that January comes. Reality returns. However joyful Christmas makes you, you can't live in December for ever.

But imagine if Christmas could be rescued from the stress or sadness of just getting through Christmas. Imagine if January could be rescued from the disappointment if your joy was in getting to Christmas. Imagine if there were a joy that lasted—that endured through January and that wasn't dented by reality. That kind of joy would be worth finding, wouldn't it?

And Christmas does offer that kind of joy. It's to be found, very simply, in getting it. Not in grasping hold of the Harrods version of Christmas—the tinsel, the tree and the traditions—but grasping hold of the events and the meaning of the first Christmas.

The people who experienced that first Christmas and understood its meaning found a joy that did not fade. So can you. Whether you're a get-to-er or a get-through-er, if you get the meaning of the first Christmas this Christmas, then you'll get the feeling of joy, and find it's a feeling that lasts. *That* joy is what this book is about.

WE THREE KINGS OF ORIENT AREN'T

J esus was born.

That's how Matthew, one of the eyewitness biographers of Jesus, sums up the event. You can tell he's a guy. There are no details of the birth weight, or the length of the labour, or how the mother, Mary, was doing, or whether the child had his mother's nose or his grandfather's eyes. Just "Jesus was born".

But there's a reason for this, beyond Matthew being a guy (and for the record, I have no idea how much my kids weighed when they were born). And the reason is that Matthew, who became a close friend of Jesus once he had grown up, is more interested in the *meaning* of the events than in all the *details* of the events.

So the only detail he gives us is the name of the baby. And even that is because this name means something. Nine months before Jesus was born, his mother,

Mary, had fallen pregnant. That's very normal! But her fiancé, Joseph, wasn't the father. Still, that's not exactly unique. But what happened to Joseph next was not at all normal and it was utterly unique:

> *An angel ... appeared to him in a dream and said, "Joseph son of David, do not be afraid to take Mary home as your wife, because what is conceived in her is from the Holy Spirit. [If this is where you think it's clearly a fairy story, and wonder how anyone could believe this really happened, have a flick to page 61.]*
>
> *"You are to give him the name Jesus, because he will save his people..."*
> *(The Gospel of Matthew, chapter 1, verse 21)*

The name "Jesus" means "God rescues". And "rescue" is a one-word summary of the meaning of Christmas. You rescue your Christmas from just getting *through* it, and from merely getting *to* it, by *getting* it—by getting the fact that it's a rescue story.

FINDING JOY

In this book, we'll focus mainly on what happened "after Jesus was born in Bethlehem in Judea, during the time of King Herod" (Matthew 2 v 1). It's going to be about what happened when "Magi from the east came" to Judea, a small Roman province on the eastern edge of the Mediterranean Sea.

We don't know very much about these "Magi". The first line of the famous carol tells us that…

We three kings of orient are…

But in fact, we don't know that there were three of them. We don't know that they were kings—magi were wise, learned astrologers. We don't know they were from the orient. In fact, that first line contains almost as many assumptions as it does words. I suppose that "We indeterminate number of learned ones from somewhere a fair way to the east of Judea" didn't scan very well.

What we do know, because Matthew tells us, is that these Magi had followed a star that they believed indicated that a "king of the Jews" had "been born" (v 2).

We do know that they went first to the capital of the Jewish nation, to Jerusalem, and were directed onto Bethlehem, a small town 4.4 miles from Jerusalem, by some religious experts.

We do know that they travelled on to Bethlehem and found the star "stopped over the place where the child was" (v 9).

We do know that when they realised they had found this boy they thought was a king, "they were overjoyed" (v 10).

And we do know that they didn't turn up empty-handed:

> *They saw the child with his mother Mary, and they bowed down and worshipped him. Then they opened their treasures and presented him with gifts of gold, frankincense and myrrh. (Matthew 2 v 11)*

And those gifts tell us why the meaning of Christmas can be summed up in that one word, "rescue".

The gold tells us what we are rescued *from*.

The frankincense tells us what we are rescued *for*.

The myrrh tells us what we are rescued *by*.

These gifts tell you everything you need to get the message of Christmas, and to feel overjoyed by the message of Christmas, just as the Magi did.

Let's unwrap them.

THE GIFT OF LEADERSHIP

In some ways, it was the most bizarre, inexplicable journey.

Some so-called wise men saw a new star in the sky. From that, they concluded that a king of the Jews had been born. You might think that a strange link to make. But far more strange is what they decided to do next.

They went to find him. And when they did, the first present they gave him was gold—a present fit for their king.

Why would these Magi, from the east, from a long way away, have bothered to come and see a baby boy who they thought was the king of a small province of the Roman empire, ruling over the Jews, a defeated subject people of the Romans? This is a bit like Theresa May phoning Donald Trump in Washington DC and Vladimir Putin in Moscow and saying,

> *"Donald, Vlad, I know we don't always get on together that well, but I think it's very possible that the exiled heir to the throne of the Maldives has been born. We must drop everything right now and go find this new and disputed king of a completely irrelevant country and pledge allegiance to him. Donald, scramble Air Force One. See you there in a few hours."*

Why would the Magi care about "the king of the Jews" being born, when they live nowhere near Judea and have nothing to do with Judea?

It's because of the promises made about him.

PROMISES, PROMISES

It wasn't only the people of Judea—the Jews—who knew of the Old Testament and the promises God had made over the centuries. Others, too, knew of what the God of Israel, the God of the Jews, had promised through his prophets, his messengers. In the ancient world, it was no secret that his promises all centred on the coming of a king of the Jews—of a "Messiah" (or "Christ"), a chosen ruler. God had been planning the first Christmas for centuries, and he had announced many of the details.

That's why when King Herod, the Romans' puppet king of Judea, heard about this other "king of the Jews", and asked where he would be, his religious advisers didn't have to scratch their heads and guess. "Bethlehem," they immediately answered—because that's what a prophet, Micah, had said six centuries before:

> *But you, Bethlehem, in the land of Judah, are by no means least among the rulers of Judah...*

Why not?

> *... for out of you will come a ruler who will shepherd of people Israel. (Matthew 2 v 6)*

And those religious advisers would have known how Micah's message had continued:

> *Therefore Israel will be abandoned until the time when she who is in labour bears a son, and the rest of his brothers return to join the Israelites. He will stand and shepherd his flock in the strength of the* LORD, *in the majesty of the name of the* LORD *his God. And they will live securely, for then his greatness will reach to the ends of the earth. And he will be our peace. (Micah 5 v 3-5a)*

Micah was talking about a king who was also a shepherd—a king who would provide for his people as a shepherd led his sheep to good grass, and who would protect his people as a shepherd drove off predators. He was telling of the coming of a shepherd-king whose rule would end up stretching to the ends of the earth and who would have the strength and the majesty of "the LORD", which is the Bible's name for the God who made the stars with a word and who sustains every atom in existence.

Micah was doing something mindblowing. He was sketching out a job description for this ruler that only the divine can fit. Who has God's strength? Only God. Who has God's majesty? Only God. Who can make a promise six hundred years before they keep it? Only God. Who was the ruler, the shepherd, who would be born in the normal way, through the agony of labour?

God.

At the first Christmas, God came from heaven, as a human, to be the King of humanity.

LEADERSHIP MATTERS

If the last couple of years have taught us anything, it is that leadership matters. The day after the 2016 US presidential election, I was on a plane from London to Boston. No American on that plane that day thought that the leader their nation had chosen was irrelevant to their lives, their hopes, their safety and their futures. Some of them were overjoyed, because they had what they had voted for, the one they were trusting to deliver their hopes. Some of them felt the opposite, and were dealing with fear and crushed hopes. But none of them thought it wasn't important.

Leadership matters. But actually, none of the candidates standing for the presidency were the leader the people on that plane needed and wanted and hoped for. Sooner or later (and usually sooner), politicians disappoint us. Whichever way that election had gone, the president would have proved imperfect, flawed and limited. We don't find the leader who can carry our hopes, deliver our dreams and bear our burdens on any ballot paper. But we *do* meet him at the first Christmas.

Here he is, born in Bethlehem. What kind of leader is this? Micah tells us. First, he can "shepherd his flock in the strength of the LORD". He can deliver. Nothing can stop him extending his rule or executing his plans. Second, he is leading his people towards a future where they "will live securely". They will experience a life with no anxiety, or concerns, where there is safety and justice and fairness. And third, "he will be [their] peace". He has come to bring the experience of living at peace with the God who made us, and made us to enjoy knowing him; of living at peace with ourselves in our minds and in our bodies, with no regrets or nagging fears; and of living at peace with others, with no family rows at Christmas, no empty chairs at Christmas tables, no divorces or pawn shops in January.

Here is a ruler with an eternal country, whose

immigration policy is to welcome anyone who will pledge allegiance to this King, regardless of their background or their past; and whose policy is to keep out all suffering, frustration, fear, and even death. This is the experience of life that everyone in the world is searching for and striving for, one way or another. At Christmas, we are being introduced to a King who brings strength and security and peace, coming into this world to beckon us into his kingdom beyond this world, and into a life that we will never find in this world. His name is Jesus.

GLIMMERS OF PEACE

Or at least, that's what the Magi thought. They thought this child was a king, and gave him an appropriate gift—gold. But then, we all tend to think too much of or hope too much of babies. And in the six hundred years between Micah's prophecy and the Magi's arrival, countless children had been born in Bethlehem and not one of them had proved to be this Shepherd-Ruler. It was a bit of a long shot to assume this particular child was any different. The gift of gold may prove only that the Magi were not as wise as everyone thought.

Who knows whether they were still alive when, three decades later, Jesus began to show that their thinking was, in fact, spot on.

Maybe news reached them of the disappearing

disease. When Jesus met a man with the incurable and usually fatal skin disease of leprosy, he…

> *reached out his hand and touched the man. "I am willing [to heal you]," he said. "Be clean!" Immediately he was cleansed of his leprosy. (Matthew 8 v 3)*

Perhaps the magi heard about the storm that stopped. Jesus was asleep in a boat rowed by some of his friends, including Matthew, some of whom were experienced fishermen. Such a fierce storm blew up that those fishermen were utterly terrified, because they knew they were about to drown. Then Jesus…

> *got up and rebuked the wind and the waves, and it was completely calm. (Matthew 8 v 26)*

Possibly, someone informed the Magi of the showdown on the shore. When Jesus landed after stopping the storm, he was confronted with two men whom evil forces held in a vice-like grip. These men were so violent that no one could come anywhere near them. But Jesus simply said, "Go" to those evil forces, and they left, leaving the men well and right-minded again (Matthew 8 v 28-32).

Who knows whether the Magi got word of the defeat of death—of the moment three days after Jesus' life had ended in his execution when the tomb where his corpse had been laid was discovered to be empty. Jesus' friends had seen him stop a storm but they had no expectation that he would rewind death. So the corpse-less grave was confusing for them, and early reports of him being alive again sounded like nonsense. But then they themselves saw him, touched him, ate with him. Then they heard him spell out what they should have grasped by then, given that they were listening to a man who had given himself life beyond his own death:

> *All authority on heaven and on earth has been given to me. (Matthew 28 v 18)*

We don't know whether the Magi heard of any or all of those episodes in Jesus' life that Matthew records in his biography. But if they had, they would have known what to make of them. This was the divine Shepherd-Ruler they had met all those years before. Here he was, proving that he was the all-powerful King, and showing glimmers of the kingdom that he had come to invite people into—a life of strength, security and peace, without disease, beyond the storms, free from fear and evil, beyond even death.

They had given that boy gold, a gift fit for a king. He had given them himself—the gift of a perfect leader.

I AM THE CAPTAIN OF MY SOUL

So far, so wonderful. Except that not everyone saw it like that. The people who'd seen Jesus drive evil out of those two guys...

went into the town and reported all this, including what had happened to the demon-possessed men. Then the whole town went out to meet Jesus. And when they saw him, they pleaded with him to leave their region. (Matthew 8 v 33-34)

The King turns up. The King does what no one else can do, restoring those men and the town they had terrorised to security and peace. And the people of that town say to that king,

Please leave.

And so do we. It may sound strange—it *is* strange—but something inside each of us wants to hold this Ruler at arm's length. We'll face the storms ourselves. We'll fight our fears on our own. We'll build a society that overcomes evil without him. We'll walk into the face of death without him.

For better or for worse, we adopt the message of "Invictus", the famous William Ernest Henley poem, as the motto for our lives:

I am the master of my fate,
I am the captain of my soul.

When it comes to my life, I am the captain. I am not going to be a mere crew member on the SS Laferton. I will take the wheel and plot the course. Jesus can be part of my crew if he wants. He can even stand next to me on the bridge and make suggestions about my direction, for me to consider. I'd quite like him to show up to fix any damage to my boat caused by the wear and tear of the voyage or by my own mistakes. But I am the captain, and so there isn't really room for another captain, even one who calms storms and can plot a way through death.

Jesus can be a teacher, a guide, a counsellor, a prophet, a philosopher. He can be anyone he likes, except who he is. Because he will not be my King.

And so when Jesus shows up, Christmas after Christmas, knocks on our door and says, *I came. I came to be your Shepherd-Ruler. I came to give you the life you want and the joy you're searching for,* we say (if we even bother to get up and answer the door), *No thanks Jesus. Please leave.*

YOU CAN'T CALM THE STORMS

There is only one problem with living like this. It doesn't work. You and I cannot calm storms or live without fear. If history teaches us anything, it is that humanity, whether individually or collectively, cannot build peace, cannot find security, and cannot banish death. Even when we fix one thing, we tend to do so in a way that causes some other problem.

One of the most famous Christmas Days in history is the one in 1914, when soldiers from Britain and Germany put down their guns and played football between the First World War trenches in France (rumours that England played well but Germany won on penalties have never been verified). It's often mentioned as an example of humanity's desire for peace and friendship. But don't forget—it happened during the bloodiest conflict the world had ever seen, a war declared by humans on humans.

It is a tragic reminder of the gap between our aspirations as humans and our abilities as humans— of the fact that humanity is no good at ruling itself, and will never be able to rewind death. How many of the players in that football match were still alive the next Christmas? How many are still alive today?

It's the same on the smaller stage of our own lives. Which of us can say we've never hurt someone else—never been so busy seeking our own satisfaction in life that we haven't pushed others aside, put others down, or produced sadness and tears and heartache instead of smiles and joy and hope?

Rejecting the rule of Jesus is natural, but it's also damaging to those around us. And it's very dangerous for us too, because God gives each of us what we choose. If we won't have Jesus as our King in this life, we won't live in his kingdom on the other side of death. If we choose to ask Jesus to leave us alone now, he will leave us alone for ever. We'll face an eternity of storms and evil on our own, without help or any prospect of it; without happiness or any hope of it. If we search for joy by asking Jesus to leave, we will find only joylessness, hopelessness and pointlessness in an existence outside his kingdom of strength, security and peace.

CHRISTMAS COMES TO LIFE

This is what we need to be rescued from—from the decision each of us have made, and continue to make, to ask Jesus to leave so that we can be the captain of our own soul and the ruler of our own life—the attitude that the Bible calls sin. We need to be rescued from the consequences of our decision.

When you realise this, the first Christmas comes to life, because when you realise this, you read these lines and you feel a deep hope and a dawning joy:

> *You are to give him the name Jesus, because he will save his people from their sins. (Matthew 1 v 21)*

The divine Shepherd-Ruler came. The Magi were right to give him gold. He showed glimmers of his kingdom and he invited people to join him and enjoy him. But he did more than that. He came not just to rule, but to rescue. He came to rescue you from your sin and its consequences.

Christmas is about rescue. It's a rescue that you and I desperately need, and can wonderfully have.

THE GIFT OF FRIENDSHIP

The December when I was 16, my girlfriend ditched me days before Christmas. I responded in a mature, level-headed way. Since my life was over and I would never be happy again, I sat in my room with the lights out and the curtains drawn and listened to Mud's Christmas hit on repeat:

> *I'm going to be lonely this Christmas, without you to hold,*
> *Lonely this Christmas, lonely and cold.*

I did that for about a day, till it got boring and I realised that no one else had noticed and that there was a party to go to that evening. At that point, I decided to be OK.

But it turns out that whenever Mud's unhappy chorus comes on the radio in December, a lot of people are nodding sadly (and with much better reason than I had) as they hear those words:

I'm going to be lonely this Christmas … lonely and cold.

Loneliness is cold. And it's by no means only elderly people who experience this. A quarter of people aged 25-34 will feel lonely this Christmas; 10% of millennials will spend Christmas alone. Almost as many have considered taking their own life because of the festive period, according to research done by the UK charity Mind in 2016. The generation that is more connected than any before is also more lonely than any before.

The chances are that if you're reading this and you're not alone this Christmas, you know someone who is; and that someone sitting fairly near your house is. And we don't even have to be alone to be lonely—often, the loneliest place is a crowded room, and that rule holds true at Christmas too.

We are often lonely, and we are often restless. One 24-year-old woman who spoke to Mind's researchers put it like this:

> *I find Christmas a particularly anxious time. Every year, there is extra pressure to be happy, to have love surround you—and for me, it feels the loneliest because of this. The media create this "perfect" vision of a family Christmas—and it's an ideal that has hung over me and made me very miserable.*

That's a downbeat way to start a chapter. It's not exactly brimming full of comfort and joy. Yet it's reality. We are relational people, but at Christmas we feel all too keenly that in many ways we're restless, lonely people.

Which is why the second gift the wise men gave the baby is such good news.

PERFUME FOR THE BOY

Frankincense—perfume—is a great gift to give to a grown woman, but a strange present for a small boy. Again, it's pointing to something significant. In this instance, "We Three Kings of Orient Are" gets it right:

Frankincense to offer have I,
Incense owns a Deity nigh…

For centuries in Judea, that was the meaning of burning perfume to create a sweet-smelling cloud. Incense said, *The Deity is near—God is here.*

When the Magi showed up in Jerusalem on their journey to discover the baby who had been born King of the Jews, they most likely would have seen the city temple. In truth, it was hard to miss. The most imposing building in the city, the complex was built using blocks weighing up to 100 tons each, and it measured around 1500 feet by 1000 feet. A workforce of 10,000 laboured on it. Unsurprisingly, though it was still unfinished when the Magi visited, it was already widely considered one of the wonders of the ancient world.

Yet what was most special about it was not how it was built so much as who lived there. For the temple was where God had made his home, among people. The temple was where heaven came to earth. The temple was where God invited people to come and be at home with him. If you had been alive in 100 BC, the place where you would get closest to God was the temple in Jerusalem.

And in the temple, incense burned day and night. It burned on a specially-built "altar" that was placed exactly where God had instructed, because this was the place where, he said, "I will meet with you" (Exodus 30 v 6). And God had said that his chief priest, who was in charge of keeping his home just as he wanted it, must...

> *burn fragrant incense on the altar every morning when he tends the lamps. He must burn incense again when he lights the lamps at twilight so that incense will burn regularly before the LORD for the generations to come. (Exodus 40 v 7-8)*

At the Queen's London residence, Buckingham Palace, if the flag bearing her Royal Standard is flying, the Queen is there. It's just a piece of material, but it is a visual message: the Queen is here, in her home. And in God's Jerusalem residence, in the temple, if the incense was burning—and it always was—God was at home. It was just perfume, but it was a visual, and smellable, message: God is here, in his home.

Now, why the guided tour of a first-century city?

To realise how strange it is that, when the Magi turn up in Jerusalem, they keep hold of their incense. It's still in their baggage when they reach Bethlehem. They don't offer it at the temple. They offer it to the baby.

The frankincense points to the promise that in Jesus, God was coming to make his home with us. God was coming to offer relationship to us. And—whether we know it or not—that is what each of us is looking for and longing for. It is the answer to the experience we all have, some of us from time to time and some of us every day... the experience that 24-year-old girl feels at Christmas... the experience that one ancient writer, a man named Augustine of Hippo (which was his home town, not his shape), summed up this way:

Our hearts are restless...

And he's right. All of us are restless, striving to get what we think will satisfy us in life. But whatever we gain or grasp, deep down there's always a sense that there might be more and that there should be more. It's the reason that celebrity magazines are not filled with happy-ever-after stories of how I got famous... got the Oscar... got the gorgeous guy/girl... got the beach-ready body only three days after giving birth to perfect twins... got lasting joy. No, along with the success stories, and often *following* the success stories in individuals' lives, are the restless-ever-after stories— stories of divorce and desperation and despair.

WHEN ALL YOUR DREAMS COME TRUE

In a way, there's only one thing worse than not achieving your dreams, and that's achieving them—and finding that they don't give you what you'd hoped. The author Jack Higgins was once asked, "What do you know at 60 that you wished you'd known at 16?" His answer: "I wish I'd known that when you get to the top, there's nothing there."

Or, as Ed Sheeran put it in "Eraser":

> *I chased the pictured perfect life, I think they painted it wrong ...*
> *Ain't nobody wanna see you down in the dumps*
> *Because you're living your dream, man, this should be fun.*

There's nothing there... I think they painted it wrong. So often the people with everything find that they have everything except whatever it is that they really need. Bob Geldof—the man who wrote the Christmas classic "Do They Know It's Christmas?", which has raised tens of millions for those who will be physically empty this winter—describes this sense of restlessness, of spiritual emptiness, in his usual bluntly poetic way. When he was asked if he felt fulfilled, here's how he responded:

> *Not at all—I don't know what that would mean. I'm unfulfilled. Otherwise why are these large holes here [Geldof thumps his chest.] I'm frightened of it. It*

> *makes me very depressed so I stay active, frenetically so,*
> *and that allows me to think I'm not wasting my time.*

Large holes in here. Our hearts are restless. So what's the answer? That fourth-century thinker, Augustine, had discovered an answer—the answer. He was actually writing a prayer…

> *You have made us for yourself, and our hearts are*
> *restless, until they can find rest in you.*

Augustine had learned the lesson of the frankincense—that we are made to enjoy one relationship above all others: a relationship with our Maker, with our God. Without that, there'll always be a gap, and since it's a divine-sized gap, nothing that we pour into it—money, fame, beauty, sex, influence, helping others, nothing—will come close to filling it. Augustine had experienced the joy of the frankincense—that in Jesus, God has made relationship with himself available to anyone, no matter who they are, where they're from, what they've done. This is what Christmas rescues you for—for friendship with God.

THIS UNIVERSE IS WARM

This is wonderful news, if it's true. It means that the universe is not pointless and pitiless. It means life is not about joining the chase for more and more stuff to fill your life and sate your appetites, a race in which most lose and the most unfortunate win, because they're the ones who find there's nothing much there. A godless universe is ultimately a lonely, cold place, a dog-eat-dog world in which all the dogs die.

But this is not a godless universe. And so you need never be alone, even if you're the only one sat at your table this Christmas. You need never feel empty, even if this life has given you none of what you hoped it would. You need never feel you are wasting your time. That's what relationship with God offers.

The birth of Jesus reveals God to us, and opens the way for relationship with God for us. What Jesus reveals is that God is a God of relationship—there is one God containing three persons, all fully God and all different. We call them the Father, the Son, and the Spirit. In divine mathematics, 1+1+1 equals 1.

That's mind-boggling. I can't get my head round it. But it would be a very disappointing God who could be fully explained by my human mind, or by yours. In fact, that god would be a human-sized god—no god at all. The God of Christmas is bigger and better than any god we would come up with ourselves.

God is God the Father (who, confusingly, we often just refer to as "God"). He made and announced the Christmas plan, as we've seen. God is God the Son. He was born as a human as the centre of the plan, as a baby called Jesus. God is God the Spirit. He worked the plan by enabling the eternal God the Son to be conceived as a human baby in Mary's womb. And he works the plan still today by opening people's eyes to get the meaning of the events of the first Christmas, and enabling people to discover the joy of getting Christmas.

That's the one God in three persons, who we meet at the first Christmas. And what holds these three persons of the Trinity together is... friendship. The kind of loyal, committed, enjoying-each-other's-company friendship that the best of human relationships point to. The heartbeat of the cosmos is infinitely satisfying relationship. At the heart of reality is a God of friendship, who invites each of us to experience and enjoy his friendship. This universe is a warm place.

COME HOME

Six Decembers ago, I met Terry. He was a nice guy. Funny, with a twinkle in his eye and a great love of Chelsea Football Club and seconds of pudding.

Two Decembers ago, I went to his funeral. Terry was a drinker, and he drank himself to death. He only felt himself when he was on the bottle. And in his chase for the next drink or six, he'd pushed his family away, he'd pushed his friends away, he'd lost his job and his health and his hope. He had nothing left because he had no one left. He hoped his wife might return to him, but it was too late. He longed for his kids to trust him, but it was too late. He wanted his friends to respect him, but it was too late. I've never seen a man so crushed by his own mistakes as Terry was. He was empty.

It's easy to feel pity for him. But you and I are not so different. In our chase to feel ourselves, to fill ourselves, to find ourselves, we've pushed our God away. We may achieve great things and accumulate wonderful things, but there will always be a hole in our lives that is God-shaped, and can be filled only by him. We make our personal universe a godless place, and then wonder why we're lonely and restless there. Deep down, whether or not we try to suppress the feeling of it, we're empty.

But it's not too late—because "incense owns a Deity nigh". Jesus came to rescue us *from* our rejection of him, *for* relationship with him. He invites us to walk in friendship with him, to come home to God by inviting him to make himself at home in our lives. The wise men's gift to Jesus was incense. Jesus' gift to you is what the incense pointed to—a relationship with him, the relationship you were made for. There's no need to be restless, no need to feel the chill of loneliness this Christmas. Your heart can find its rest in the warmth of relationship with God.

THE GIFT OF A CLEAN START

The Christmas Day I was eight, I gave up at 5:40am.

It had been a particularly emotional run-up to Christmas that year, and therefore an especially sleepless night. All I wanted for Christmas was the Subbuteo football game. It was top of the wish-list that I had handed my parents.

My parents, however, had said they would buy me socks. Just socks. I was sure it was a joke. Wasn't it?

At 5:40am, awake and unable to sleep, I could bear it no longer. I gave up counting sheep, crept downstairs and searched through the presents under the tree for the one, or ones, my parents were giving to me. It took a while. There was just one. It was small, and squashy. I peeled the sticky tape off and peeked through the gap in the wrapping paper.

It was socks. And I sobbed.

When everyone else got up, I held it together (because creeping downstairs to open presents in the night was highly illegal) until breakfast, when I broke down.

"You got me socks," I confronted my parents: "And I don't want socks. Why would I want socks? I want the football game."

They smiled. It turned out I should have checked under the sofa. There, wrapped up, was a large, Subbuteo-game-shaped box. The socks were a joke.

I think my parents found it all quite funny. I didn't.

OFFENSIVELY PERFECT

I would guess that Mary and Joseph felt something similar about the last present the Magi gave their small son. Myrrh was a liquid used for pain relief in extreme circumstances (like impending death) and for embalming bodies after death.

And here these strange men were, giving Mary and Joseph myrrh—for their infant son. It would be like having a baby today, and in the midst of opening up the gifts of cute clothes and fluffy teddies, you start unwrapping a large box, it's wooden, and… it's a coffin. For your child.

You can imagine Mary being tempted to say to the Magi: "Thanks for coming all this way. But you got him myrrh. And he doesn't want myrrh. Why would he want myrrh?"

Myrrh is such an offensive birth gift. It's saying, *Your baby is going to die.* It's so inappropriate.

And yet, for this boy, it was perfect.

The sad truth of this world is that every child who is born will die. But this baby was different—because Jesus was born in order to die. It was always God's plan that the one who lay on the wooden planks of a food trough would one day hang off the wooden beam of a cross.

Joseph and Mary couldn't have known it as the Magi offered them this weird, unsettling, borderline offensive present. Maybe they kept it in their house for years, up on the shelf, unused, usually ignored, but occasionally pondered upon before the matter was pushed to the back of their minds again. After all, it was just a gift, and the gold and the frankincense had been strange in their own ways too.

But then their son grew up and began to do things only the divine Shepherd-King could do. What the gold promised had come true. And then he began to invite people into friendship with him as their God. What the frankincense promised had come true. The myrrh on the shelf was proving harder to ignore…

And then it became impossible to ignore, as Jesus was arrested, tried, found guilty of doing something the details of which were hazy but which everyone agreed definitely merited death, and was nailed to a cross to die. Perhaps as his mother stood before her son, watching him breathe his last, her mind returned to that strange moment when the wise man had stretched out his hands to place before her young son that third gift. That myrrh. For a corpse. Which is what she was now looking at.

YOU CAN MAKE ME CLEAN

Perhaps the myrrh was a strange comfort at that point—because it showed that what happened to Jesus was no accident. It had been part of the plan since his birth—since well before it, in fact. The Shepherd-King had always been intending to die for his subjects.

But why?

Back in chapter 2, we briefly met a leper who Jesus healed. That leper's experience is a key that unlocks why Jesus died, because leprosy among God's people was not just a physical problem—it was also a spiritual one.

Leprosy was a disease that was an outer sign of an inward reality—a symbol of sin. Not that a leper was any worse or better than anyone else—after all, there was and is no one who has not decided they will captain their own ship and ask Jesus to keep his hands off the tiller of their life. But leprosy was a sign that all was not well with the world because people had sought to shut God out of his world. And so lepers were not allowed to come to the temple—to the one place in the world where all was well because God was at home there. A leper could not come to the place of the burning incense, to the place where relationship with God was offered. Lepers were separated from what they most needed, distanced from where they most needed to be.

This may all sound quite strange to our 21st-century ears. But see it as a huge, unmissable visual aid. Just as the incense was a thrilling visual reminder of the relationship with God that every human was made to enjoy and needs in order to know real joy, leprosy was a sobering visual reminder that no human was able to enjoy that relationship, because they were covered with the spiritual disease of sin.

So you can imagine the hope tinged with desperation in that leper as he came and knelt before Jesus and said:

> *Lord, if you are willing, you can make me clean.*

And you can imagine the joy as Jesus answered him,

> *"I am willing … be clean!" Immediately he was cleansed of his leprosy.*

Jesus was willing and Jesus was able to clean him, to wipe away all that prevented him from coming to the temple, so that he could enjoy relationship with God.

But Jesus did not heal him just by speaking to him:

> *Jesus reached out his hand and touched the man. "I am willing," he said. "Be clean!"*

No one touched a leper, because leprosy was contagious. Touching a leper made you unclean. Touching a leper meant that you, too, were unable to enter the temple and instead had to stay at a distance, separated from God. In touching this man Jesus was himself becoming unclean—yet in doing so, Jesus made the man clean.

And that is what Jesus is willing to do for us too. As he hung on the cross, he cried out:

> *My God, my God, why have you forsaken me?*
> *(Matthew 27 v 46)*

He knew the answer. For the first and last time in all eternity, the perfect friendship at the heart of the universe—the perfect love between the Father, Son and Spirit—had been severed. On the cross, the Son knew the abandonment of living in a godless personal universe—knew the loneliness, the emptiness, the restlessness of that existence. He was separated from relationship with his Father. And he was suffering that for you, so that he could take the dirt of your sin and make you clean. The perfect, pure, sinless King was treated as though he were imperfect, dirty, sinful.

Here's what Jesus was doing on the cross. He was reaching out and saying to you, *Because I am God I am able, and because I love you I am willing, to experience the future outside my kingdom that you have chosen, in your place.*

I am willing to be covered in sin and separated from my Father, so that you can be cleaned of your sin and come into friendship with my Father.

Jesus took the eternity we have chosen so that he could give us the eternity we need. And then he rose back to life so that he could rule that eternity.

The gift of myrrh shows us that we can't make sense of Jesus' birth or of Jesus' life if we have not made sense of Jesus' death. You can't get Christmas if you don't get Easter. Jesus' greatest gift to us is his cleanness. We are rescued *from* our rejection of God, we are rescued *for* relationship with God, and we are rescued *by* the death of God.

STAY OUTSIDE. COME IN.

When I was a kid, I played football most lunchtimes at school. My speciality was slide-tackling. My only real ability was to tackle, preferably the ball but failing that the man, and then kick the ball as far away from my goal as I could. I am basically a walking explanation for England's repeated footballing failures. But still, I was good at sliding. So by the end of lunchtime, I would be covered in mud. It wasn't quite clear where I ended and the mud began.

It was great fun, but the problem was that my mother had told me not to. Or at least, not to play in my school trousers, and to get changed into tracksuit trousers and old trainers. But I couldn't be bothered to get changed. No one else did. Maybe today I would stay on my feet. Maybe today I wouldn't get muddy.

But I always would, and I would walk very slowly on the way home. Sometimes I'd stop and try to wipe the mud off my trousers (and jumper, and shoes), but succeed only in moving the mud around rather than removing it entirely.

Eventually I would get home, and Mum would open the door and look at me and utter the two words beloved of mothers with sports-mad children the world over:

Stay outside.

And the door would close and I would stand, muddy and in the cold, outside the nice warm, clean house. Because I was muddy, I could not be warm. But then the front door would open and Mum would come back, and with a variety of cloths and towels and a bucket of water she would peel off my outer clothes and wash me until the mud was gone and I was back to being me. Then she would hand me fresh, clean, warm clothes to put on. And then she would say…

Come in.

And then she would say, *Please don't do it again.*

When God looks at us, he does not see people who can come into the warmth of his house. His kingdom is perfectly pure, and those of us who have spent our lives sliding around in the mud of our rejection of him are told…

Stay outside.

But wonderfully, Jesus comes outside to us, with everything that is needed to clean us up, and he wipes us and he gives us new, clean clothes to wear, and then he says…

Come in.

THE JOY OF THE MYRRH

And this is where you discover joy—not just in a house in Bethlehem, but ultimately at an execution site near Jerusalem. Because Jesus has cleaned you up, you can come before his perfectly pure Father as a perfectly pure person and enjoy perfect relationship with him. So many of us are trying to avoid God, ignoring him or redefining him or just staying clear of thinking about him because we know, deep down, that we are not good people. We put on a front, we smile with our family at Christmas, but we know in our more honest moments that there are things we've done and things we've not done that *we* don't find acceptable, let alone God.

So many of us are worried about God, unclear and anxious about whether when we turn up on his heavenly threshold, we'll be clean enough to get in. We try to remove our mud, but we just move it around. We try to turn away from doing wrong, but it proves too ingrained to avoid it for long. We try to wash away the bad by doing good, but mud sticks. In our prouder moments we assume we're good enough; in our more honest ones we worry that we're not. Deep down, we wonder whether we have cleaned ourselves up sufficiently to be allowed into eternity. The cross says, *You haven't... and you can't... and you don't need to.*

There is great joy in being able to be honest about yourself, and knowing you're forgiven. There is great joy in knowing that God knows the worst about you, and loves and accepts you anyway, because he already dealt with the dirt. It's liberating.

It frees you to stop avoiding God. It frees you to stop worrying about God. It frees you from having to pretend. It frees you to be honest with yourself, with God, and with others, rather than getting defensive or despairing whenever your carefully-constructed façade of goodness is challenged. It frees you to be able to forgive others' failures, rather than harbouring bitter grudges that eat you up, or plotting bitter revenge that separates you from others. That's the joy found in accepting that God should say, *Stay outside*, but in discovering that, through Jesus' death, he says, *Come in.*

That's the joy of the myrrh.

FINDING A HAPPY ENDING

Everyone likes happy endings. But the first Christmas doesn't have one.

Nativity plays do. Last year I went to my son's school nativity. It was a wonderfully-managed logistical exercise, and it finished with a stage full of thirty donkeys, thirty cows, two dozen angels, a smattering of shepherds, three wise men wearing crowns (the scriptwriters had clearly based that part on "We Three Kings of Orient Are"), Mary, Joseph and Jesus (well, a doll).

The costumes were great. It was very sweet. I loved it. But it had ignored the final scene:

Having been warned in a dream not to go back to Herod, [the wise men] returned to their country by another route. When they had gone, an angel of the Lord appeared to Joseph in a dream. "Get up," he said, "take the child and his mother and escape to

Egypt. Stay there until I tell you, for Herod is going to search for the child to kill him." So he got up, took the child and his mother during the night and left for Egypt, where he stayed until the death of Herod. And so was fulfilled what the Lord had said through the prophet: "Out of Egypt I called my son."

When Herod realised that he had been outwitted by the Magi, he was furious, and he gave orders to kill all the boys in Bethlehem and its vicinity who were two years old and under, in accordance with the time he had learned from the Magi. (Matthew 2 v 12-16)

The Christmas story does not end with the Magi bowing and a small boy receiving gifts. It finishes with a king murdering and small boys dying.

I don't know how you react to this final scene in the Bible's account. Personally, I think it's good that this massacre is here—not good that it happened, but good that it's here. It helps remind us that the Bible's story is not sentimental; it's historical. And the past reality of this world, like the present reality right round the world and in our own lives, is a mixture of joys and sadnesses, of ups and downs, of triumph and tragedy. Our Christmases are the same. And so it's a relief to find that the Bible gets that. The Bible is not an escape from reality, it's a book about reality. It's about the cries of a newborn baby and the cries of grieving mothers. It's about the real world.

And in reality, "the one who has been born king of the Jews" demands a response. No one around back then heard the news and had the option of not responding. A king heard. Some religious experts heard. The Magi heard. And their different responses show us that we all have three options when it comes to reacting to that announcement that the Shepherd-Ruler, promised by Micah in 600 BC, was born in (roughly) 0 BC.

THE KING

Why does the Christmas story end in a massacre? Why did Herod dislike Jesus so much that he wanted to kill him, and why was he prepared to kill any number of boys just to be sure he'd taken out this particular one?

The answer is that Herod was the captain of his soul. He was the master of his ship. In his particular case, his ship had a large crew, since it covered a whole country. He was king, and it had taken a lot of blood (mainly other people's), sweat and scheming for him to reach the top of the greasy pole. And he had made it. Judea was his. This was, as Matthew puts it, "the time of King Herod" (v 1).

But now another king of the Jews had arrived. And ultimately, Judea belonged to him. No one has a greater claim to rule than Jesus, the divine Shepherd-King. After all, he made the world in the first place. Herod didn't.

So Herod had a decision to make. Would he accept ruling under Jesus, or would he seek to rule over Jesus? He chose option two—to resist Jesus, fight Jesus, so that he could carry on being the only ruler. That's why Bethlehem's young boys were massacred. The action of mass murder was motivated by Herod's attitude of refusing to let Jesus be his ruler—of saying, "I am the master, the captain—not you."

I AM THE MASTER

Now, Herod had a country to rule. I don't. But I do have my own life. It's mine. I rule it. Except if Jesus is the Shepherd-Ruler, the Messiah, then actually my life belongs to him. He made me. I didn't. We can't both be in charge, and so my natural reaction—everyone's natural reaction, in fact—is to resist Jesus' claim so that I can continue to rule. As far as each of us is concerned, Jesus can be whoever he likes, except who he is—the King.

That doesn't lead us to ruin people's lives through committing mass murder. But our refusal to let Jesus be our ruler does lead us to ruin others' lives in smaller, less noticeable ways. The people we've taken for granted. The people we've taken advantage of. The people we just used, for our own ends or enjoyment, until we got a better offer. The people we've snapped at, shouted at, ignored or belittled. The little things we do each day, and don't do each day, which make the lives of those around us a bit less or a lot less satisfying than God wants them to be.

All those are signs of an inward attitude that looks at our life and looks at Jesus and says, *Actually, I am the master of my fate, I am the captain of my soul. You will not be in charge round here, Jesus. Please leave.* And that's what Herod said, and that's how Herod acted.

But he was wrong.

Herod was not in control. God was, and he ensured that his Son was safely in Egypt when Herod's soldiers started knocking on the doors of family homes in Bethlehem. As it turned out, Herod was not even the captain of his own soul:

> *After Herod died, an angel of the Lord appeared in a dream to Joseph in Egypt and said, "Get up, take the child and his mother and go to the land of Israel, for those who were trying to take the child's life are dead." (Matthew 2 v 19-20)*

After Herod died. Only one king is still alive at the end of this final act of the historical Christmas, and it is not the one who killed those children. Death is the final scene in every life, and it strips our power and mocks our pretensions.

We can actively and angrily resist Jesus' claims. You can put this book down now and walk back into your life and spend it firmly holding Jesus at arm's length, telling him to leave every time he knocks at your door. You can spend your time ripping apart the arguments for his existence and his claims to be God, mocking those who follow him, building your own kingdom. You can do all that. But death will still be the final scene in this life, and beyond it you will not be master of your soul, and your ship will not be headed for a safe, secure, peaceful eternal harbour.

THE PRIESTS

I think Herod is a tragic figure in many ways— furiously resisting the one who had come to give him everything he'd ever really needed. But in many ways, the religious experts are even more tragic. Let's rewind the story a little:

> *After Jesus was born in Bethlehem in Judea, during the time of King Herod, Magi from the east came to Jerusalem and asked, "Where is the one who has been born king of the Jews? We saw his star when it rose and have come to worship him."*
>
> *When King Herod heard this he was disturbed, and all Jerusalem with him. When he had called together all the people's chief priests and teachers of the law, he asked them where the Messiah was to be born. "In Bethlehem in Judea," they replied, "for this is what the prophet has written:*

'But you, Bethlehem, in the land of Judah,
　　are by no means least among the rulers of Judah;
for out of you will come a ruler
　　who will shepherd my people Israel.'"

Then Herod called the Magi secretly and found out from them the exact time the star had appeared. He sent them to Bethlehem and said, "Go and search carefully for the child. As soon as you find him, report to me, so that I too may go and worship him."

After they had heard the king, they went on their way, and the star they had seen when it rose went ahead of them until it stopped over the place where the child was. (Matthew 2 v 1-9)

The chief priests and the teachers of "the law" (the law that God set down for his people in the Old Testament part of the Bible) were experts. They knew every detail of every promise God had made. So they knew exactly where the Messiah—God's long-promised, all-powerful King—would be born: Bethlehem.

But they didn't go to Bethlehem.

They heard a claim that the king who they claimed they'd been waiting for their whole lives had been born. And they did... nothing. They were told that God's great Shepherd-King was 4.4 miles away—just a couple of hours' journey. And they did... nothing.

After the Magi headed off on their journey towards joy, the priests would have carried on reading their Bibles. They would have gone into the temple. They would have smelled the incense. But they never met the one the Bible speaks of, the one the incense points towards. They never met Jesus.

Maybe they were just too busy. There were temple jobs to do, religious rituals to follow, a king to advise. Maybe there just wasn't time to drop all that in order to go see a small child in a nothing town.

It's possible to be very religious and completely miss the point. In fact, it's possible to use religion as a way of ignoring Jesus. When our religion is about what we do, it keeps us as the master of our own fate. We can very politely ignore the truth that we need God to come and clean us up. We can very politely get on with covering our dirt with a layer of goodness. We can go to church this Christmas. We can go to church every Sunday. But that is not the same as meeting Jesus and being cleaned up by him.

There are lots of Herods around, aggressively and angrily resisting Jesus. Some of them write books. Some of them troll others on social media. Most of them just mock the Christians they know, internally if not out loud. Maybe you're one of them.

But there are far more priests around, politely but insistently ignoring Jesus. Very happy for others to find him. Very happy to be busily religious, or moral, or good. Very happy to sing the carols. Even very happy to hear about the events of the first Christmas, and think about them, and acknowledge the truth of them, and do… nothing. Very happy to sail on into eternity, holed below the waterline.

THE MAGI

Let's have a happy ending to this chapter:

> *After [the Magi] had heard the king, they went on their way, and the star they had seen when it rose went ahead of them until it stopped over the place where the child was. When they saw the star, they were overjoyed. On coming to the house, they saw the child with his mother Mary, and they bowed down and worshipped him. Then they opened their treasures and presented him with gifts… (Matthew 2 v 9-11)*

They bowed down and worshipped him. The Magi chose not to resist, not to ignore, but to worship. In fact, they had been choosing to worship Jesus ever since they saw that star in the east and started their trek towards Jerusalem and then the short distance on to Bethlehem. They'd been worshipping him by giving him their time, by giving him their energy and, finally, by giving him their wealth. That's what worship is— giving your all, your life, to Jesus as you put your wallet, your calendar and your mind at his disposal.

These Magi knew the King of the Jews had been

born. They sensed he was the divine Shepherd-Ruler. They had a decision to make. Resist or ignore Jesus, or worship him? Resist or ignore Jesus, or let him be the captain of their fates and the master of their souls, and discover lasting strength security, and peace, on into eternity beyond death?

They worshipped him.

And they find joy—heart-swelling, deep down, spring-in-your-step joy. They alone end Matthew's account of the first Christmas knowing what it feels like to be "overjoyed". Herod doesn't. The religious experts don't. But the Magi finish the first Christmas heading home, back to normality, with a new meaning and a new feeling—with a joy that lasts, and that will never end.

THEY COULD
BE ANYONE

C.S. Lewis, who wrote *The Lion, the Witch, and the Wardrobe* and the other Narnia books, became a Christian in his thirties. He described himself as "the most dejected and reluctant convert in all England". In many ways and for quite some time, he had fought hard against Jesus. He did not want to give up the rule of his life and his soul. But in the end, he gave in to the beauty and truth of the one who lay at the centre of the first Christmas and hung on the cross at the first Easter. He worshipped "him whom I [had] so earnestly desired not to meet".

And when he wrote his autobiography describing how he had met Jesus and begun to worship him, he called it…

Surprised by Joy.

Maybe you're not at that point yet. Maybe this little book has given you much to think about, and some more questions to get answers to. Let me encourage you to keep searching for joy. Let me urge you to keep looking at Jesus to see if he is the source of that joy. One great way to do that is simply by reading one of the four historical biographies about him—the Gospels of Matthew, Mark, Luke and John. Another is to speak to someone you know who knows him. A third is to visit a website like christianityexplored.org.

But maybe you are where C.S. Lewis was— perhaps with a sense of reluctance, perhaps with a sense of relief, perhaps with a mixture of the two. Maybe you're experiencing what Lewis called "the steady unrelenting approach of him whom I so earnestly desired not to meet". You're beginning to get Christmas—that its meaning is rescue, a rescue from your rejection of God, a rescue for relationship with God, a rescue by the death of God. You're beginning to see that true joy is found not in getting to Christmas, or in getting through Christmas, but in getting Christmas—in grasping its meaning and experiencing its feeling.

You're on the threshold of discovering joy that lasts, of finding the life that you've been looking for. You're facing the decision the Magi did, and C.S. Lewis did, and actually that everyone does—whether to allow Jesus to be the captain of your soul and the master of your fate.

Will you speak to him now as your King and ask him to rescue you from your rejection of him, for relationship with him, by his death on the cross to clean and forgive you? Will you worship him?

We don't know very much about the Magi. And that's the point. They are outsiders, they are unknowns, and they stand for anyone—no matter who they are, where they are from, what they do or what they have done—anyone who realises that the promised Shepherd-King has come, and who chooses to worship him and to ask him to rescue them.

There is a surprising joy in worshipping King Jesus. While those who try to grasp everything from him lose everything, those who love to give everything to him find everything in knowing him. That's what the Magi sense. That's what the Magi discover. They are outsiders, they are unknowns. They could be anyone.

They could be you.

PS: DO YOU REALLY EXPECT ME TO BELIEVE IN A VIRGIN BIRTH?

It's very possible that you've been reading this book with a large "But" in your mind. Perhaps you've realised that the message of the first Christmas is one that offers joy—but your problem isn't that it doesn't sound great, but that it doesn't sound true. After all, this whole story starts with something that sounds impossible: a virgin falling pregnant. And maybe that's the reason that you struggle to see any of these words as history, rather than a fairy story:

> *This is how the birth of Jesus the Messiah came about: his mother Mary was pledged [that's a legal word—in those days if you got engaged it was a legally binding commitment, just as marriage is today] to be married to Joseph. But before they came together she was found to be pregnant through the Holy Spirit.*
> (Matthew 1 v 18)

At the heart of the Christmas story—and at the heart of Christianity—is the claim that a woman who had never had sex became pregnant. How can anyone believe in a virgin birth and retain their intellectual credibility? It's a fair question. Here are three things to ponder—three reasons you can believe in the virgin birth without having to suspend your ability to think.

First, if there is a God—and of course none of us

have cast-iron proof that there isn't—then we would expect that his actions will be different from ours, more powerful than ours, and beyond any ordinary capability or comprehension. In fact, if someone wanted to prove they were God, then we wouldn't just expect him to do what we could not—we'd *demand* it.

Second, it is not impossible for somebody to get pregnant without having sex, by someone they've never even met. I have a friend who fell pregnant and gave birth in exactly that way a few years ago, because in recent years medical science has worked out how to do that. If what we're reading here in Matthew's Gospel is God at work, then he was surely perfectly capable of doing in his way supernaturally what doctors whom he's created are now able to do in their way, medically. We may not understand how this virgin conception happened, but that doesn't mean it *can't* have happened.

Third, think about what Matthew tells us happened to Joseph, Mary's fiancé. When he found out that Mary had (as far as he could see) cheated on him, he understandably decided to split up with her. Kindly, because he "did not want to expose her to public disgrace, he had in mind to divorce her quietly" (v 19).

But only five verses after that, we're told he "took Mary home as his wife" (v 24). Not only that, but "he did not consummate their marriage until she gave birth" to Jesus (v 25). You can imagine the taunts and what people would have said to him and about him: *How*

weak, Joseph, to accept her into your home after what she's done!
How could you fall for that ridiculous story Mary's spinning about
the father being God! And you're not even sleeping with her? Are
you mad, Joseph? And yet this man, who had decided to
split up with her, ends up marrying her.

How do we explain the complete change in this
man? It must have taken something extraordinary!
Matthew agrees:

> *An angel of the Lord appeared to him in a dream and*
> *said, "Joseph son of David, do not be afraid to take*
> *Mary home as your wife, because what is conceived in*
> *her is from the Holy Spirit." (Matthew 1 v 20)*

What it took was an angel from heaven coming to
explain that this was a virgin birth because the baby
was the Son of God, come from heaven. It's an
extraordinary, but not an impossible, explanation
for Joseph's extraordinary turnaround. I'd argue that
when we start to think about it, the virgin birth at the
beginning of Jesus' earthly life—just like him rising
from the dead at the other end of his time in this
world—becomes not less plausible, but more.

This is the wonderful thing about the Christian
faith. It happened in history, and while it involves
mystery that we cannot understand, at no stage does
the Christian message demand that you suspend
your ability to think. This rescue story is not just
wonderful. It is also, crucially, credible.

thegoodbook
COMPANY

BIBLICAL | RELEVANT | ACCESSIBLE

Thanks for reading this book. We hope you enjoyed it, and found it helpful.

Most people want to find answers to the big questions of life: Who are we? Why are we here? How should we live? But for many valid reasons we are often unable to find the time or the right space to think positively and carefully about them.

Perhaps you have questions that you need an answer for. Perhaps you have met Christians who have seemed unsympathetic or incomprehensible. Or maybe you are someone who has grown up believing, but need help to make things a little clearer.

At The Good Book Company, we're passionate about producing materials that help people of all ages and stages understand the heart of the Christian message, which is found in the pages of the Bible.

Whoever you are, and wherever you are at when it comes to these big questions, we hope we can help. As a publisher we want to help you look at the good book that is the Bible because we're convinced that as we meet the person who stands at its centre—Jesus Christ—we find the clearest answers to our biggest questions.

Visit our website to discover the range of books, videos and other resources we produce, or visit our partner site www.christianityexplored. org for a clear explanation of who Jesus is and why he came.

Thanks again for reading,

Your friends at The Good Book Company

UK & EUROPE	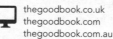 thegoodbook.co.uk	0333 123 0880
NORTH AMERICA	thegoodbook.com	866 244 2165
AUSTRALIA	thegoodbook.com.au	(02) 9564 3555
NEW ZEALAND	thegoodbook.co.nz	(+64) 3 343 2463

 WWW.CHRISTIANITYEXPLORED.ORG
Our partner site is a great place for those exploring the Christian faith, with a clear explanation of the good news, powerful testimonies and answers to difficult questions.